SHOWING OFF

The Lighter Side of Show-Jumping

SHOWING OFF

The Lighter Side of Show-Jumping

Julian Seaman

Designed by Harold King

First published in Great Britain in 1986 by Robson Books Ltd.,
Bolsover House, 5-6 Clipstone Street, London W1P 7EB.

Copyright © 1986 Julian Seaman

British Library Cataloguing in Publication Data

Seaman, Julian
    Showing off: the lighter side of show jumping.
    1. Show Jumping—Anecdotes, facetiae, satire, etc.
    I. Title
    798.2'5   SF295.5

    ISBN 0-86051-397-1

Typeset by Bookworm Typesetting, Manchester.
Printed in Great Britain by Redwood Burn Limited,
Trowbridge, Wiltshire.
Bound by WBC Bookbinders Limited, Maesteg.

Contents

Acknowledgements

The author has gathered material for this book from many sources and people. Among the books consulted are: *Bedside Jumping*, Harvey Smith (Willow Books); *Caroline Bradley - A Tribute*, Malcolm Severs (Harrap); *Dead Lucky*, Lionel Dunning with Alan Watts (Arthur Barker); *Horseman's Handbook to end all Horsemen's Handbooks*, Rintoul Booth (Wolfe Publishing); *Harvey Smith on Show-Jumping*, with Victor Green (Pelham Books); *Jump for Joy*, Pat Smythe (Cassell & Co); *Jumping* (Naldrett Press); *Modern Horsemanship*, Colonel Rodzianko (Seely Service & Co); *One Jump Ahead*, Pat Smythe (Cassell); *Pigsticking*, Willy Rushton (Macdonald & Co, Publishers); *Ryan's Master, The Story of John Whitaker*, Jane Fuller (Stanley Paul); *The Edgars Forever*, Ann Martin (Pelham Books); *The Forward Impulse*, Piero Santini (Country Life). Grateful thanks to all these, Katie Colvin, Jane Ratcliffe and Tracy Baker, to *Private Eye* for the Maddocks cartoon on page 38 and the Woodcock cartoon on page 68, to the London Standard for the Jak cartoon on page 48 and to Syndication International for The Wizard of Id strips. Thanks also to Mike Williams for his cartoons.

Findlay Davidson and Peter Hogan have kindly lent photographs.

Foreword

BY RAYMOND BROOKS-WARD

Some of us who read Julian Seaman's *Horse Laughs* waited in fear and trepidation, and some with eager anticipation, for him to take the lid off show-jumping. We were not disappointed – from the first fence Julian's bubbling sense of fun sweeps you along over the twisting course.

If you want history it's there, from the start in Paris in the 1890s to the present day. However, this is like no other historical record; take the International Horse Show of 1909 at Olympia, confined to troop horses, chargers and hunters. One competitor summed it all up: 'poles that flew like cricket stumps, a ten-day spree entertaining our girl friends at the Show.'

Riders come in for some light-hearted comments. Harvey Smith on David Broome: 'Basil hates to be kept waiting in a restaurant which means he gets served last.' There are also some magic quotes: 'When a fall is imminent we cannot prevent it; if we could, aviation would be child's play' or 'The art of riding is keeping a horse between you and the ground.'

In the nearest equivalent to a horsey *Private Eye*, Julian looks at the other side of show-jumping: who went out with who; drugs for horses that didn't work; after-care in the bath for some riders; the true story of the famous V-sign, and various other character assassinations, including mine!

Seaman has many sides to his character which come through: writer, cartoonist, micky-taker and poet – yes, poet. How about this for the first verse of show-jumping: 'Pat Smythe became the heroine Of little girls on Ovaltine.' He has dared to take the dignified, serious and classical art of show-jumping apart. In return I will let you into the secret of this formidable author:

Scene I   The Adelphi Breakfast room on race day. The redoubtable amateur jump jockey J. Seaman having his customary bottle of champagne.

Scene II   Aintree Race Course. 'They are off, Julian Seaman flying along at the back. Fence No. 1, J. Seaman on the floor.'

Seriously, I commend this book to all who like to learn and laugh. I hope that he turns his attentions elsewhere – feelings probably felt by some of those who feature in the book who could be forgiven for saying this young man should go far, the further the better!

★ ★ ★ ★ ★ ★ ★ ★ ★ ★ ★ ★ ★ ★ ★ ★ ★ ★ ★ ★

Colonel Mike Ansell: 'If fifteen years ago any person had considered the publishing of a book on show-jumping, he would have been thought to have taken leave of his senses.'

Colonel Mike Ansell, from his foreword to
Showjumping, 1954

★ ★ ★ ★ ★ ★ ★ ★ ★ ★ ★ ★ ★ ★ ★ ★ ★ ★ ★ ★

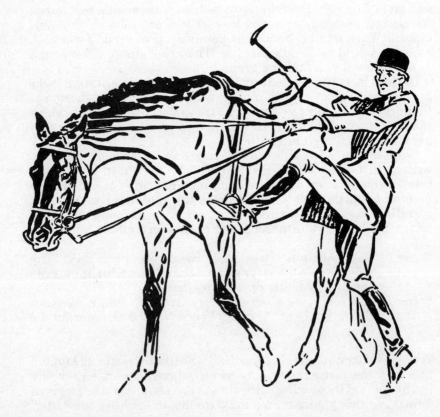

THE WAY WE WERE

People actually only thought about jumping horses in Britain 300 years ago when the open farming system was changed by a series of Enclosure acts. The fences which this produced forced hunters to learn to jump.

The first known show-jumping contest was held in Paris in 1866 at a harness show. The riders did a little show in front of the stands then disappeared across country over the obstacles. Understandably the crowd found this somewhat dull, so the following year all the jumps were put into the arena and a sport was born.

When jumping first arrived in England at the end of the last century it was known as 'lepping'. (Though Ted Edgar would probably be less than impressed if he thought his yard today would be described as a lepper colony!)

In the early days show-jumping courses consisted of little more than a few hurdle and brush fences, and the rider's performance was judged on style. Then there came an occasional gate, wall, and sometimes water. The water jump was often given more points for being jumped well than all the others put together!

Because of the wonderful ostentation at the first Olympia Show in 1907 — a horse ran out at a jump depositing his rider, who totally disappeared in a bank of hydrangeas — the show itself was a great success but not surprisingly a financial flop.

In a review of the second Olympia show of 1908 in the *Livestock Journal*, one jumping class was written up: 'Class 133. Over the course. None but officers in uniform were allowed to compete in this class, which was productive of some remarkably good performances, the Englishmen doing very well upon their rather untrained mounts.' In fact, not one British rider was in the top 13 places!

Old jumping courses were a standard one and a half times round the arena, down the centre and out.

An early British pioneer, Major-General Geoffrey Brooke, was one of the first to realize the importance of dressage training for jumping.

TRUE FACTS

Nipper, one of the top American show-jumpers of the Fifties, was originally a French horse called Honduras – he was captured from the French by the Germans, and from the Germans by the Americans.

Many of the best show-jumping horses have had a history of being 'difficult' when young. It seems to show that they have spirit, which if channelled the right way tends to put them above the more mundane and 'easier' mounts.

Uncle Max, the horse on which Ted Edgar won the King George V Cup (in one of the two years when the show happened outside on the hallowed football pitch at Wembley), previously spent four years in America as a bucking bronco.

One of John Whitaker's good horses, Novilheiro, was bred in Portugal for bull-fighting. He was then brought to England and became a dressage horse. Former European Horse Trials Champion Rachel Bayliss then evented him for a while before his true vocation as a jumper was realized.

The Dunning's horse, Roscoe, started life as a bucking bronco in Australia, where he had killed a man. On the way to the abattoir he jumped out of the rail truck and for months wandered round the small Australian town, until he was taken by an Aborigine boy. The boy hired him out to gallop round the town, and then sold him to another Aborigine who started to jump him. He was then bought by Australian rider Jeff McVean, who brought him over to England, where the Dunnings bought him, through their owner Tony Elliott, almost immediately.

Jungle Bunny was a big, black, decidedly difficult mount and was thus named after Lionel Dunning, in a fit of temper, had referred to him as 'this bloody crazy jungle bunny'. It took the authorities some time to accept this as an official name, since it was thought it might upset the race relations lobby.

HORSES

In his early days Jungle Bunny would jump almost anything apart from blue walls. So eventually Lionel Dunning had to invest in some practice walls and pots of blue paint to iron out the problem.

A horse of another colour . . .

Lord Lonsdale, the instigator of the first International Show at Olympia in 1907, had such a craze for the colour yellow that he extended his obsession to buying pale chestnut horses with white socks – which since time immemorial have been considered quite the worst sort.

Pep talk

There have been instances of 'fixing' horses where tests have shown that various drugs have been administered to horses to dull their performances. Unlike racing, however, there is little scope for 'pepping up' a horse, because the increased 'pep' is likely to cause carelessness. Someone did discover that cocaine helped to increase a horse's accuracy and care, but the amounts of the drug needed to have any noticeable effect on a half-ton horse was so prohibitively expensive that it made it a totally unviable way of cheating.

You can lead a horse to water . . .

Cruelty to horses, though it quite rightly attracts press attention, isn't rife, since a horse is unlikely to perform well if it is not enjoying its job. The senior riders make sure that if they see a newcomer mistreating an animal they intervene.

. . . but mind what he drinks

'Don't drink the water' is the saying when going to strange parts of the world. Riders take heed of this and often take purifying pills with them on international trips to ensure that their horses, as well as themselves, don't suffer.

"Well. . .do something!"

As the Everest team would say, 'That'll be Jim with the wind.'

Saddle sore and smelly, a bitter end for Ted n' Nick

Harvey Wallbanger

The modern horse box caters for all competitors' needs

1. **Sleeping area**

2. **Kitchen**

3. **Separate lavatory**
   (riders no longer have
   to go to the Luton)

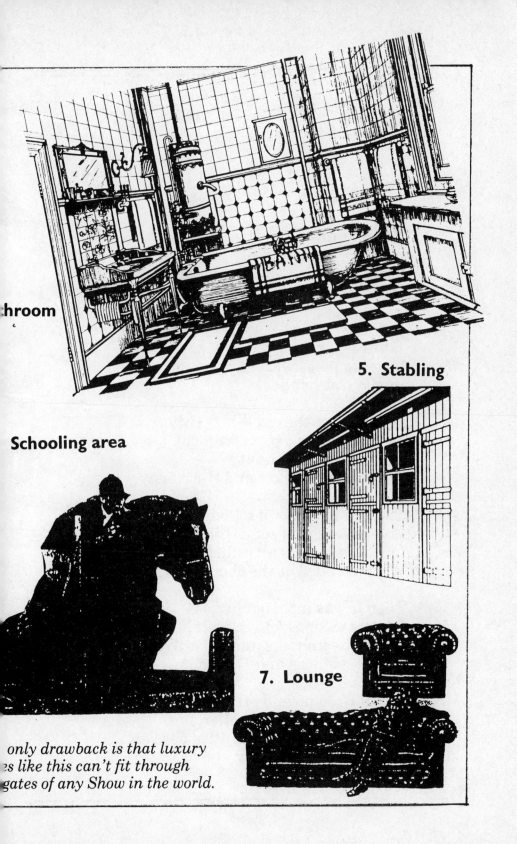

hroom

Schooling area

5. **Stabling**

7. **Lounge**

only drawback is that luxury
es like this can't fit through
gates of any Show in the world.

POETRY CORNER

With apologies to Sir John Betjeman

Brought up on the District Line,
In Richmond, a suburb sublime,
Pat Smythe became the heroine
Of little girls on Ovaltine.

In those teams with Harry Llewellyn
Winning prizes every week,
Leaping poles with gay abandon –
In 1950, at her peak.

Moments at the old White City:
Memories don't seem far away
Of Tosca, Hal, Finality,
At Richmond Show and Harringay.

Those early days of television –
Live coverage of something new;
In sitting-rooms all round the country
We marvelled at the chosen few.

Then it was into the Sixties,
Beatles, Stones and Superstars,
When the jumpers jumped at Wembley,
Harvey Smiths and Ted Edgars.

David Broome and Mr Softee,
Marion Coakes on Stroller, too,
How we watched enthralled as ever,
As Pegasus the horses flew.

Then came both the Schockemöhles
Eddie Macken, Boomerang,
Hickstead Banks and hackamores –
On and on the start bell rang.

Round and round the same old circuit
Same old riders rode and won
David Vine enthusiastic –
Till snooker came and spoilt the fun.

SHOW JUMPING

Like three-day eventing, the British are rather good at this, in spite of the efforts of the British Powers That Be who forced a large number of our best to turn pro, Harvey Smith and David Broome to name but a huge few. The theory behind this was that we British (fair play, the game's the thing, it's not cricket, jolly sporting, the world admires a good loser, blast, we've lost again!) felt it was time to clear up the muddled business of 'shamateurism' in the equestrian sports. In eventing and dressage, of course, they don't need the money and in racing itself the issues are more clear-cut, but in show jumping, particularly when the telly seized upon it as a ratings-puller, and threw in David Vine and a hotted-up Mozart, it became less obvious who was doing what and for how much.

If, thought the British authorities, we muck *ourselves* out, then, as is ever the case, the world will follow our fine example. Thus purified and looking good, they waited for the world, shuffling uneasily as the Germans filled their jack-boots with gutteral laughter and the Italians roared into their vermicelli. And so it came to pass that we turned out the Twelfth Men in Montreal on horses they'd never met. Once again it was a lady jumper, sweet Debbie Johnsey who saved our purple face and further persuaded me that if I hear one more coy, chauvinistic reference to 'jockettes', (a coy, chauvinistic reference to lady jockeys and not a breed of ball-twisting

underwear), from another racing commentator, I shall so place his microphone that the only sound emerging from him for the rest of his days will appear to be that of hippopotami rutting in a muddy water-hole. One place where woman has shown her equality, indeed on many occasions her superiority, is with a horse between her legs. But when you look at the brouhaha surrounding lady newsreaders or the first Sikh traffic wardenesses or Mother Thatcher you begin to wonder when man became such a silly bitch. Perhaps it's the fact the media pay more attention to firsts than lasts. For example, on the last day of the Roman Empire, the headlines would have read 'First Lady Gladiator comes Second'.

Show jumping is a cracking spectator sport, because you know what's going on all the time. You can see the poles flying, and there's a decent clock in the top right-hand corner. Some of the contests can whip you into a fine lather. I've been known to bite through the neck of a bottle during the puissance.

I imagine sponsorship is what caused the British voice of authority to have its attack, it's caused and causing conniptions all over the place, but if you can happily and without blushing name an event or race or competition after those who forked out the necessary why on earth can't the competitors enter the ring mounted on 'Bognor Regis Building Society' or 'Treadwell Wall-To-Wall'. There might be occasion for complaint if Harv

Smith rode in on 'Maltdrains Old and Nasty is the Beer to Make You Whistle', but Dorian Williams could handle it. He is extremely dexterous verbally. His patriotic fervour may go a little far at times, but I've heard him bewail our national weakness at the waterjump. We tend to fall down, or at least put a foot in the water. 'Oh, the British and water!' he will cry, and granite-like he who will not weep with him.

On the subject, however, of sponsorship, and it will rear again no doubt, television needs sport, sport needs television, both need money and the money needs both, and the Olympics needs all three.

How to be a show jumper and excite young girls at Wembley Baths

It all starts at the pony club. Frenzied mini-Shockemöhles on small, fat ponies belting over tiny obstacles, legs flapping, elbows akimbo, mothers screaming while Thelwell sketches and Shire-horsey ladies whinny and retired cavalry officers bellow like geldings fresh from James Herriot's teeth. Thence it's a long haul to Hickstead. In more ways than one as I discovered from an idle chat with Harvey Smith who while deadly on horseback and a pleasure to watch and indeed to drink with (hell to wrestle with, I would imagine),

seems to spend more time on the motorways of Europe, driving his enormous mobile home than actually engaged in jumping fences. I refrained from asking him what the correct procedure is if one of your horses falls out of an upper bunk on an autobahn.

To succeed you have to start young (good-bye, then). You must also possess a 'natural seat' and a wonderful sense of balance. (Several of those standing at the back have just fallen over.) It's expensive again, it costs from £1000 to £1500 per annum to keep a show jumper. That's more than a wife, but then, I suppose, it's probably larger. You will also need a keen sense of direction. My geographical bump is the envy of many, but I still marvel at the ease with which the jumpers find their way round, especially against the clock. I can only too plainly picture myself going backwards and forwards over the rustic gate searching vainly for the next left turn while hooters hoot and Raymond Brooks-Ward does his impersonation of Dorian Williams and vice versa. Bring up the Mozart, and exit left at gallop.

PEOPLE
Tittle tattle . . .

Raymond Brooks-Ward's best gaffe while commentating on TV was when he was describing a round by Caroline Bradley on Marius: 'Just watch this clever little stallion screw in mid air.'

The show circuit is so hectic that dates can get muddled. At one show the Whitakers could hardly believe they were the first to arrive. They were, by a whole week.

In his early days with ponies John Whitaker split his head open while trying to vault on in 'Indian' style. The pony trod on his flared trousers!

Despite the mileage horseboxes have to travel, they are not always too reliable. One year Harvey Smith had to miss the first day of a show in Berlin while his horses were stuck at Helmstadt. On the journey back from that show the wheel of the Dunning caravan sheered off on the Zeebrugge-Antwerp autoroute and they had to wait till morning before all was fixed and they could continue home. Another Dunning caravan split in two on the A13 and had to be abandoned at the roadside.

Dorian Williams boobed when, commentating on a dreadful hat worn by a duchess in the Royal Box, he forgot to switch off his microphone.

Ronnie Massarella, the British Team Manager since 1969, always insists that at least four of his six riders at any international show are present at official functions – however deadly they may be. At one such reception Harvey Smith was rather less than pleased to be greeted by the British Ambassador's wife, who enquired if he was part of the tennis team.

On the way to the Berlin Show Caroline Bradley's lorry broke down in the middle of the infamous Berlin Corridor. She arrived at the show fourteen hours later.

TV commentator David Coleman's daughter Anne was a former British champion who married jumper Tony Newberry.

At one stage David Broome went out with Judy Boulter, who is now married to Malcolm Pyrah.

The only time Lionel Dunning deliberately 'threw' a class was when he didn't want to jump off, so that he could be back in time to take out Pam Coldron to a party - Pam is now Mrs Dunning.

During the war Pat Smythe was evacuated from Richmond and stayed with the Drummond-Hays, where the future Badminton and Queen Elizabeth Cup winner Anneli was still a baby.

Long before she was married to him Pat Smythe referred to her future husband Sam Koechlin as 'a tall, curly-haired law student from Basle who seemed to live largely on grapefruit and black coffee.'

The very last passage of Pat Smythe's book *Jump for Joy* needs quoting in full – though it has no relevance at all to a book on the sport:
  'I have had one further point of association with the family of Colonel Llewellyn. Some years ago I made the tragic mistake of becoming engaged to Harry's son David. I remained his fiancée until 1953, when the blow fell.
  Without warning, without pity, David broke the silence one summer afternoon – "I've got another fiancée now; you're too old" – David will be nine next birthday.'
  Dai – the 'seducer of the valleys' – obviously started young!

Pat Smythe was at school with the actress Dorothy Tutin.

At a show in Vienna the riders were asked to a very smart Viennese ball in a château. Since all the guests were in white ties and costumes the riders felt somewhat underdressed, but the liquid hospitality made up for this. Ted

Edgar felt a bit hot, so removed his jacket. This was obviously 'not done', and a small official came up and told Ted so. Ted reacted verbally, but the Austrian could obviously understand every word he was saying. The British contingent were politely asked to leave. The following day Ted won the main class and was silently presented with his prize by the small Austrian with whom he'd had the altercation the previous night. It turned out he was the President of the show.

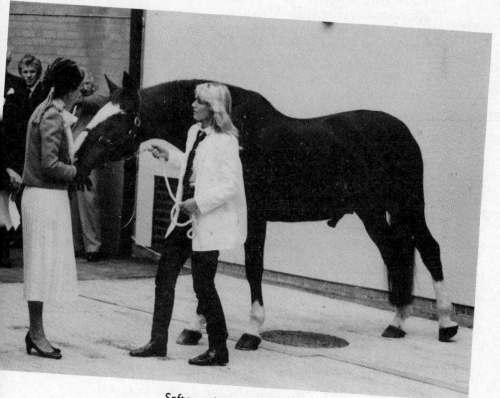

Sefton enjoying a nob's visit

An Irish martingale keeps the reins apart so that an Irishman knows which is which.

HORSES
Manely tailpieces . . .

More horses and ponies are involved in show-jumping than there are racehorses in training.

The string of horses left by German rider Hartwig Steenken after he was tragically killed in a car crash included Goya, the top puissance horse now ridden by Fritz Ligges; Gladstone, Hugo Simon's World Cup winning mount; Deister, now Paul Schockemöhle's top ride, and Wallaby, ridden with such success in speed classes by Liz Edgar and Nick Skelton.

Harvey Smith's Sanyo Music Centre was related to Specify (which won the National) and also to Jungle Bunny.

Pat Smythe's great horse Flanagan had previously competed at Badminton, where he was ridden by Brigadier Bolton.

Stroller – a 14.2 pony. European Ladies Champion 1970. Silver Olympics 1968. Died Monday 24 March 1986 aged 36 and was buried on the front lawn of Marion Mould's house.

Paul Schockemöhle's horse Deister jumps brilliantly out of doors but tends to get over-excited when jumping in closed spaces such as Wembley. Paul gets round this by stuffing cotton wool down his ears to cut out the razzmatazz. We are yet to see show-jumpers wearing blinkers!

Paul Schockemöhle's horse Deister nearly lost an eye in a lorry crash in which one German team horse was killed.

All three of Eddie Macken's first top rides, Pele, Oatfield Hills and Easter Parade belonged to his trainer, Iris Kellet, who herself had twice won the Queen Elizabeth Cup and had been European Women's Champion in 1969.

Eddie Macken's brilliant horse Boomerang was at one stage owned and brought on by the Edgars. Liz won about fifty classes on him before eventually the horse returned to his familiar rider.

A titled lady reputedly turned up in her role as sponsor's wife at a White City show with her own supply of champagne concealed under her voluminous frock.

According to Harvey Smith, David Broome can't stand being kept waiting in restaurants, and because of this tends to upset the staff, with the end result that the service is slow anyway.

Harvey ascribes David Broome's pin-point accuracy as a rider to the fact that he's not the bravest of jockeys – 'He's like a brilliant boxer who doesn't want to take a punch.'

Ted Edgar was expelled from school at the age of 13 for smoking. He offers the excuse that he was already heavy for his age and was trying to keep his weight down. Oh yeah?

TIES: The all velcro white tie — sticks like a limpet to your chest to avoid embarrassing flap as you clear Puissance Walls — stain resistant & fire proof. £10.00
Ties & Bondage, Bath (none in stock (get it)).

HATS: You too could be described as a veteran member of British teams if you wear the patent 'Robeson'® faded grey riding hat. Available in three shades: grey, light grey and completely falling apart — or try the Paul Robeson black — very popular.
Petered-out Products, Petersfield.

ARTIFICIAL AIDS: Train your horse to jump higher with these reconstituted hedgehog skins (only one previous owner — the hedgehog). Strap them to the top of a jump and the sky's the limit — Don't be a prick buy now.
Twiggy Winkle Products, Hoggs Back, Guildford.

HORSES: Paddy O'Paddy has a selection of International horses for sale — well OK they're only International as they were bred in Ireland, but I've got just the one for your guv'nor.
BOX 69.

GROOMS: Are you prepared to wear tacky emblazoned anoraks — get up at 5.00am — not wash your hair for weeks — be told to move out of shot by David Vine and risk catching a social disease? Become a groom — apply: White Slaves Ltd, Weal Barrow, Avon, Calling.

HORSE BOXES: The ultimate in horse transport. Commissioned by Aristotle Onassis for the Greek Team and never used. This luxury ocean-going cruiser has everything an Olympian might need — completely useless but wonderful — contact: Dynasty Sales, Lesbos, Greece.

PROPERTY: Grocklands: This outstanding equestrian centre, conceived several years by the kitchen appliance magnette, Madge E. Micks has changed hands more often than anyone can remember. Everyone else has tried to run it — why don't you?
Contact: Lame Fox & Hunt Estate Agents.

TACK: You too can be commercial — Don't have a sponsor? Never mind we can paint any logo on the side of your lorry and supply colour co-ordinated attire for your team so that your 'show cred' remains intact.
Tacky Enterprises, Tryon House, You Never Know, There's Always One, Berks.

STRAIGHT FROM
THE HORSE'S MOUTH

Piero Santini, explaining why a rider shouldn't interfere with a horse's mouth when a fall is imminent: 'We cannot prevent anything falling that we are falling with; if we could, aviation would become child's play.'

'Unnecessary throwing about of arms and legs corresponds in horsemanship to ranting on the stage, a characteristic of barnstorming Thespians, never of first-class actors.'

'Were I making a list of riding "don'ts" I would certainly include getting on the horse by the stirrup, except when absolutely necessary.'

Conte R. di Campello, writing about show-jumping in Europe in 1954: 'I am not very optimistic about the future of show-jumping in Europe: but I would say that the two countries with the greatest probabilities of solving these various problems and leading Europe in equestrian activities are England and Germany. Do not ask me the reason for this opinion, as I would then have to go into history and psychology!'

In the early nineteenth century there was a sporting Squire Osbaldeston who stated that there was no fence that couldn't be jumped, provided that one quite expected to fall!

'Sitting is but one thing in horsemanship and there are thousands of things in the Art. I never knew in my life a good horseman thrown, but I have known many presumptious, ignorant fellows get falls, for it is a mistake as ridiculous as it is common to take sitting fast on horseback for the whole art of horsemanship'
William Cavendish, Duke of Newcastle, 1592-1676

Colonel Mike Ansell, in the foreword to Pat Smythe's *Jump for Joy*, writes: 'It is said that all Englishmen are born horsemen, and yet there are few sayings less true . . . without work he will never succeed.'

Major Malcolm Wallace – Director General of the British Equestrian Federation.

Artificial aids: whisky, flasks, tranquillizers, hedgehog skins etc. . . . Spurs should be used 'spurringly'.

PEOPLE
Fancy that . . .

Horses for courses

The celebrated racehorse owner Dorothy Paget also owned
show-jumpers which were often ridden by Pat Smythe.

Worzell Gummidge rides again . . .

The great equestrian theorist Caprilli tested his ideas of
'the forward seat' by using a straw-filled dummy strapped
to the saddle.

Caprilli hated writing and it was only an enforced
confinement after a riding accident which persuaded him to
dictate his ideas to his favourite pupil Biachetti.

One thing leads to another . . .

Everest Double Glazing first took an interest in show-
jumping sponsorship when one of their district managers,
off his own bat, sponsored a small event at the South of
England Show. Coincidentally one of the partners in the
company was introduced to Bob Dean — the man behind
British Equestrian Promotions, at the same time.

One of the reasons for the success of the Everest team is
that Ted Edgar, as trainer, goes to most of the shows. Very
few other trainers do this.

Behind every great man . . .

John and Michael Whitaker's father suspected the show-
jumping scene as being too circus-like. It was Mrs Whitaker
who got them keen on the sport, and John has never had
another coach.

For a brief period Harvey Smith became a professional wrestler.

Naughty Bits...

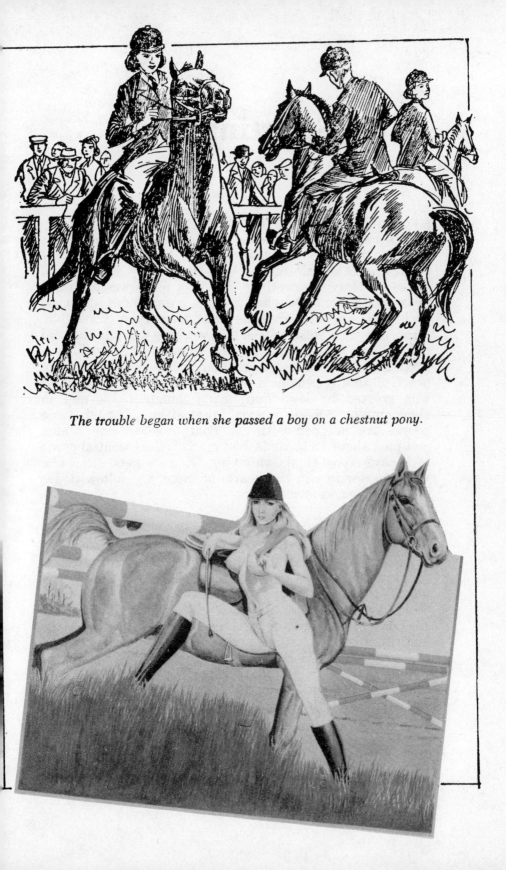

The trouble began when she passed a boy on a chestnut pony.

This Sporting Life . . .

Play up and play the game . . .

In his contribution to *How To Enjoy Jumping* (1954), Captain Wilson Stephens recalls one International Horse Show when a steeplechase jockey, Tim Molony, was riding a horse for Harry Llewellyn: 'The first fence was a simple brush but Molony ploughed through it and ended up on the deck. The reason I treasure that memory is three-fold. First, nobody wants to see a fall, yet here was one that did nobody any harm; secondly, the victim took it with such good grace (of course a chasing jockey gets plenty of practice) that it became a lesson in deportment; thirdly, it was greeted by loud and hearty laughter . . . and in showjumping nobody is ever laughed at, although some people are laughed with . . . That little episode, which occupied about 15 seconds, had in it all the essential spirit of today's type of showjumping. A man need not be a world-beater to win the hearts of those who follow it. He need only be a sportsman.'

Only here for the beer . . .

The participants at the early Olympia shows consisted of troop horses, chargers and hunters, who had done almost no preparation for the show. No one minded, especially the riders, one of whom wrote later: 'What matter if the poles flew like cricket stumps, and rustic gates turned like cartwheels, we were having a ten-day spree in London and entertaining our relations and girlfriends at the expense of the International Horse Show.'

Death with honour . . .

Winston Churchill suggested in his memoirs that one of the most honourable ways of dying was to break your neck in a fall from a galloping horse.

Breeches. 'If the curve is skimped you will look like an unsuccessful speedway rider – if they balloon outwards you will resemble a First World War aviator in a silent film comedy.' (Rintoul Booth, *Horseman's Handbook*)

'**Spurs**, incidentally, should always be worn with boots, which, without, look about as smart as evening shirts without ties.' (Piero Santini, *The Forward Impulse*)

EVERY MAN
HIS
OWN FARRIER
BY FRANCIS CLATER.

HALIFAX
MILNER & SOWERBY.

WARD'S PASTE FOR THE PILES.

TAKE—Powder of elecampane, four ounces;
Black pepper, four ounces;
Fennel seed, six ounces;
Honey, eight ounces;
Sugar, eight ounces;
Mix, and take a spoonful two or three times a day.

TO CHOOSE WATER FOR BREWING.

Use soft water, or if it cannot be procured, expose hard water in the coolers to the air, for two or three days, and throw a handful of soda into each hogshead.

WALNUT CATSUP.

TAKE—Walnut-shell juice, three gallons;
Salt, seven pounds;
Ginger, eight ounces;
Shallots, eight ounces;
Garlic, eight ounces;
Horse-radish, eight ounces;
Essence of anchovies, one quart.
Mix.

POWDER FOR HICCOUGH.

Put as much dill-seed, finely powdered, as will lie on a shilling, into two spoonful of syrup of black cherries, and take it presently.

(RECIPE, No. 87.)

ALTERATIVE BALLS FOR THE FARCY.

TAKE—Precipitated sulphur of antimony, g
guaiacum, and socotrine aloes, of ea
one ounce, in fine powder;
Nitre, two ounces;
Calomel, and cantharides, in powder,
each two drachms;
Mix, and make them into a mass for bal
with lenitive electuary. Each ball
weigh one ounce and a half.
These balls will be found useful in obstinate dis
orders, where the blood is foul: such as the far
glanders, scab, or mange, and lameness of t
joints, &c. for which one ball may be given for
fortnight or three weeks together, as may be thoug
most proper: or the following may be given.

(RECIPE, No. 88.)

COMMON ALTERATIVE BALLS.

TAKE—Nitre, roll sulphur, antimony, of each fou
ounces, in fine powder;
Ginger, in powder, two ounces;
Liquorice powder, and treacle, sufficient to
make them into a mass for balls. A
piece of the size of a pigeon's egg, or an
ounce and a half in weight, may be rolled into a ball, and given to the horse
every other morning.
N. B. In all impurities of the blood, all medi-
cines of this class, that are administered as altera-
tives, must be continued for a considerable time,
before much benefit can be expected from them.

(RECIPE, No. 105.)

ASTRINGENT DRINK.

TAKE—Tincture of catechu, one ounce;
Elixir of vitriol, two drachms;
Peruvian bark, in powder, and bole ar
nic, in powder, of each one ounce;
Tincture of opium, half an ounce;
Mix, and give it in a pint of red wine m
warm.
This drink may be repeated every other day
three times. This method of treatment wil
found very efficacious to stop purging, and i
wise to strengthen and heal the internal parts

'Pet' names . . .

At the Windsor Horse Show one year commentator Sheila Barnes announced a horse, Flash LIII (Flash the fifty-third), as Flash Lill – which has now become one of her nicknames.

Malcolm Pyrah is known to his friends as 'Hitler'.

John Whitaker is known as 'Spot'.

Lesley McNaught is known as 'Tulip'.

David Broome's nickname amongst the riders is 'Basil'.

For reasons best known to him, Douglas Bunn, who has done an enormous amount for show-jumping in Britain, both as an amateur rider and then instigator of the most prestigious jumping Derby in the world, has bestowed upon himself the title 'Master of Hickstead' – a term which even the gossip columnists are prepared to use.

Harvey Smith has been referred to in the press as 'Godzilla with spurs'.

French Nations Cup team member Hughueff Persyn had a horse with the unfortunate name of 'Pschitt'.

Ted Edgar

When he was point-to-pointing Ted Edgar used to work out in a gym in Leamington with former world middleweight boxing champion Randolph Turpin.

Alan Ball, the BSJA senior course builder, is a joiner by trade, so he is adept at working out his courses on paper before construction, unlike some international builders who wander into the arena with a few ideas and spend a couple of hours working it all out.

Harvey Smith's farm manager, Willie Halliday, was a successful amateur show-jumper and helped to establish among other horses Olympic Star (now Sanyo Sanmar).

After a contest in Cairo Michael Whitaker joined in the cabaret to reveal a hidden talent as a belly dancer.

Nick Skelton had ambitions to be a jump jockey before joining the Edgars in 1974; champion jump jockey John Francome, on the other hand, was a top junior show-jumper before going racing.

Bob Dean, the former Chairman and part-instigator of British Equestrian Promotions, the company linked to the BSJA and British Horse Society, which raises sponsorship for both competitors and individuals in the equestrian world, is the Dean of the well-known Pearl & Dean cinema advertisements.

Harvey Smith teaches some of his horses tricks. Sanyo Shining Example lies down to order, and proved a great success with the crowd at the Olympia Show in 1983 when in the fancy dress class Harvey and David Broome flopped on to him as a couple of drunks.

An occasional feature of televised shows is a jockey's jumping contest.

Pat Buckley on Lulu

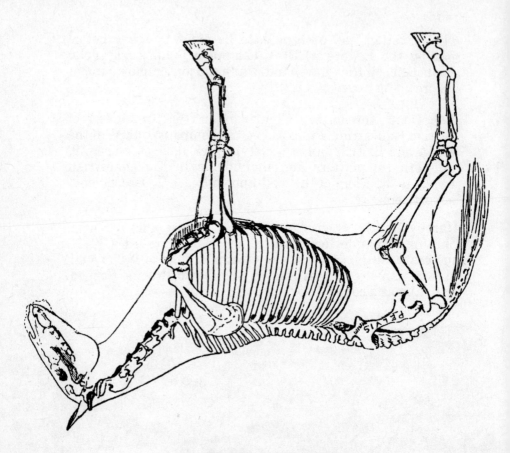

SKELETON OF THE HORSE.

A THOROUGH KNOWLEDGE OF THE HORSE'S ANATOMY IS OF THE GREATEST ASSISTANCE TO THE RIDER.

Achievements . . .

Three days before the 1963 Hickstead Derby Ted Edgar broke his arm breaking in a young horse. He had the bones put straight and put on a sling. Douglas Bunn offered him a crate of champagne if he got round the gruelling 16-fence course. Amazingly Ted finished in the money with only 8 faults.

Injured with a groin strain from the previous round, Hans Winkler had to be given morphia to ease the pain at the Stockholm Olympics where in his second round he jumped clear to secure the gold medal.

When John Whitaker started riding Ryan's Son, the horse had only won 50p. He has now won over £250,000 in prize money.

Ted Edgar rode over seventy winners point-to-pointing.

Pat Smythe won the first point-to-point she entered, in 1950, at 12-1, on a horse called Only Just.

Because of the order of jumping at the Los Angeles Olympics the Americans knew they had already won when their third member had gone. This put poor Tim Grubb on the spot as he entered the arena to help secure a silver for Britain, since the announcer decided to inform the naturally partisan crowd of the situation. The ensuing racket totally unnerved his horse, Linky, and he had a disastrous round. After this débâcle Britain were lying 6th after 3 horses. Fortunately John Whitaker only had one down, Tim's score could be discarded (only the best 3 scores count), and Britain won the silver.

The French horse Pitou had won the individual gold medal at the Mexico Olympics in the three-day event. Other eventers to make it in show-jumping were Merely-A-Monarch, which won both Badminton and the Queen's Cup for Anneli Drummond-Hay, and Hydrophane Coldstream, who completed Badminton with John Kersley and then became a jumping star with Derek Ricketts.

Disappointments . . .

One year, having been selected for a team abroad on Finality, Pat Smythe suffered the disappointment of being told by the owner of the horse, Mr Snodgrass (sic), that he wanted to keep the horse at home for his son to ride in a local hunter trial.

On Friday, 13th April, 1984 Lionel Dunning's sponsor pulled out and removed all the horses from the yard apart from the jointly-owned Jungle Bunny.

One reason why the Dunnings' sponsor pulled out was so that his horses could be eligible for the Olympics, in which Lionel and Pam couldn't complete, but as fate would have it, the horses didn't run in Los Angeles either.

"If that's Harvey Smith out in front, why isn't he doing his two finger salute!"

Sanyo HiFi not getting Hi enough at Nice.

Despite his short stocky build, it was back trouble, usually associated with tall riders, that forced Alwin Schockemöhle's premature retirement from the sport.

David Broome turned professional in 1973, signing with the Esso Petroleum company, but the subsequent oil crisis put an end to that sponsorship after only one year.

When Ted Edgar first broke his knee in a fall he sawed off the plaster when he got home and got a carpenter to make him a cradle to stop him bending his leg in bed at night. A couple of years later he smashed the other knee, kept the plaster on this time, but has never jumped in the ring since.

'Security'

SUNDAY EXTRA

MADDOCKS

"Well somebody's been drinking — I can smell it."

HORSE TRADING

Pam Dunning found a horse at Fred Welch's called Ganderbush which she thought might suit Lionel. The Dunnings, however, couldn't afford too much, so Fred let them have it cheap on the understanding that the balance would be paid if the horse ever amounted to anything. The horse is now better known as Jungle Bunny.

Pam Dunning was given the horse Miniature to ride in perpetuity by ex-Harrods boss Sir Hugh Fraser in 1975, on the understanding it would be jumped in his name. When, however, the following year Sir Hugh lost a considerable sum gambling and had to sell his horses, Trevor Banks, who bought them, insisted that Miniature was part of the deal, since the horse was still in Sir Hugh's name. Pam lost the ride.

Lionel Dunning's horse Costa Brava was bought from the Royal Marines for £150.

Pat Smythe bought a retired racehorse with tendon trouble called Fourtowns for £150 – she renamed him Prince Hal, and he turned out to be one of her best jumpers. Another of her best horses, Tosca, was also bought for the same price.

Though Caroline Bradley's mother had had a hunter before she was married, the first pony to enter the household afterwards was bought with a trap, for transport during the petrol shortage in the war years.

David Broome was 19 when he rode in his first Nations Cup in 1959 and his ex-Army horse, which cost only £60, was the leading money winner.

The great horse Anglezarke was bought by Trevor Banks for Captain Mark Phillips to ride before becoming the ride of Malcolm Pyrah.

CHILDSPLAY

A filly in the family

Liz Edgar looked after her daughter Marie for the first two months after she was born, but wanted to get back to the horses – so she employed a groom to look after Marie!

Crime and punishment

If the Whitaker boys misbehaved at home they were walloped with a yard broom.

Tally-ho!

Much as he enjoyed his first day's hunting at the age of eleven, Lionel Dunning, who started off the day on a leading rein, but was by mistake released, was sent home by the Master, Major Sir George Llewellyn Tapps-Gervis-Meyrick, for overtaking everything except the fox.

Order of the boot

Unlike the rest of his family Lionel Dunning was sent to a 'posh' private school. However, the family score was levelled when he was expelled for being a rebel.

Ignorance is bliss

'Looking back, I reflect that a babe on horseback may often enjoy the charmed safety of a reeling drunk in a city street, missing death by a hair's breadth, and with the same innocence of the danger involved.' (Pat Smythe)

Don't spoil the child . . .

'When small children have too many excitements, by the time they grow up they may get bored with things.'
                              (*Colonel Rodzianko*, 1937)

. . . or spare the rod

'When a child can manage his pony well, present him with a stick as a reward.'   (*Colonel Rodzianko*, 1937)

Horse-mad

From *The* (first!) *Pony Club Manual* (published in 1950) – on a career with horses: 'The danger of becoming "horsey". By this I [Lisa Shedden] mean that, in devoting almost all waking hours to the job, one is apt to let other interests become obscured. Some people seem to be unable to change their clothes and, for a few hours, to pretend that there is no such animal as the horse. How unnecessary this is.'

Harvey Smith

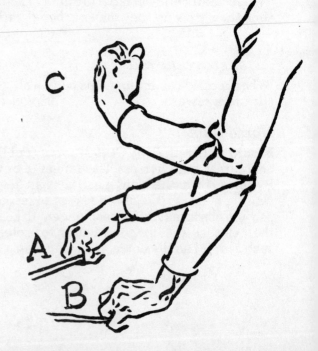

Douglas Bunn

SOME FANCY BREEDS MIGHT BE DEVELOPED FOR PETS

It will be noticed that when a rider walks the course, he carefully paces out the distance between the fences in a combination. This tells him whether his horse will need to take one stride or two strides between the elements of the combination. Normally a one-stride double is 25 feet apart, and a two-stride double, 36 feet. This distance is adjusted slightly according to the type of fences used. If a rider lands too far out over the first part of the fence then he will have difficulty in adjusting his stride for the second part — a spread fence, for instance, will take a horse further out over the first part than an upright. The horse must also land without having lost impulsion. If he hesitates before the first fence, there may be too little impulsion left to reach the next fence in stride. Combinations are testing and varied — one may have a big spread in, a small upright in the middle, and then another big spread out — presenting the sort of problem that sorts out the men from the boys.

This Sporting Life . . .

At a show in Brighton during the Fifties, Pat Smythe's horse Tosca won every day and jumped more than two hundred fences without a single fault.

The 'frog' in a horse's hoof – the V-shaped spongy bit – works as a shock absorber, but also helps pump the blood back up its leg.

One year at the Woburn Abbey Horse Show, Harvey Smith, who had just swapped one of his horses for a lurcher dog, decided to go 'lamping' rabbits in the park in a car which he had borrowed for a couple of days under the pretext that he might buy it. He only wanted to spin about the park chasing bunnies.

Liz Edgar selflessly lent her horse Jacapo to her brother David Broome to ride in the Tokyo Olympics.

Quote by Harvey Smith from his book *Bedside Jumping*: describing Harry Llewellyn – 'He's an old man now, but you still won't get much past Sir Harry.' Stand up, Dai and Roddy!

After leaving school Paul Schockemöhle went into the family business and it wasn't until he was 27 that he had time enough to devote to riding. Unlike his brother Alwin he showed no natural talent whatsoever, but despite being told this, his determination and a great deal of practice have taken him right to the top.

Commentator Raymond Brooks-Ward actually goes to the shop and buys his wife's frocks.

The V Sign

Part 1. At the Blackburn Show in 1956 some unusually high prize money (for that time) was at stake – £250, £100, £50, then nothing, for the open class. This had attracted some top riders. Only four went clear – Seamus Hayes, Alan Oliver, Derek Kent and the fledgeling Harvey Smith. A great friend of Harvey's, Sammy Morphet, had heard the other three deciding to split the prize money, whatever the outcome, not considering H. Smith a serious rival. As Harvey entered the ring, Sammy swept up a V sign and blew a raspberry, telling his friend to 'give it to them'. Harvey won, took home £250 and the others had to split £150 between them.

Part 2. Harvey won the Hickstead Derby in 1970. He then forgot to bring back the trophy the following year. In a cheeky attempt to placate Douglas Bunn he said that it didn't matter as he would win it again. Bunn was unamused. Harvey, however, was incensed when he heard cheers from Douglas Bunn's box overlooking the arena as he rolled a pole. Since all the competitors except Stephen Hadley on Prospero (who had a refusal for three penalties, and one time fault) and Harvey on Mattie Brown, had had at least two fences down, there was a jump-off between the two. Over the shortened course Prospero had three down, and Mattie Brown only two. Harvey pulled up in front of Douglas Bunn's balcony, and remembering Sammy Morphet's gesture fifteen years before, raised his two fingers.

Part 3. Five hours after the event, Harvey received a telegram from Douglas Bunn informing him that because of his behaviour he had been disqualified and would have to forfeit the £2,000 prize money. There was a BSJA enquiry. Harvey was let off, and then in front of the Press he and Douglas made it up, and as a rather different gesture Harvey donated part of his prize to Riding for the Disabled.

Nick Skelton on Everest Lastic, Olympia 1977. He cleared it for the UK record of 7ft 7⁵⁄₁₆ins at the next attempt. (In 1986 the official FEI world high jump record stood at 8ft 1¼ins, achieved by Captain Alberto Larraguibel Morales on Huaso in Santiago Chile in 1949).

Paddy McMahon wasting perfectly good bubbly on Tigre.

Ted Edgar briefly went out with Caroline Bradley.

When Liz Edgar's mother Millie Broome heard that her 17-year-old daughter was going out with the wild Ted, she nearly had a fit.

Liz and Ted Edgar got engaged on her 21st birthday in 1964.

Three years running during the Fifties Dorian Williams escorted Pat Smythe to the Horse & Hound Ball in London.

The commentator Tom Hudson has been on the receiving end of riders' pranks. One year at the Suffolk Show, while Tom was out on a binge, Trevor Banks and some helpers moved Tom's caravan so that its door was by a post and unopenable. After much trying Tom gave up and dossed on someone's floor.

Even at the important shows not everything is taken too seriously behind the scenes. Sometimes riders will organize bareback jumping contests floodlit by lorry headlamps.

Raymond Brooks-Ward's first BBC commentary job required him to wax lyrical about the mounted police playing musical chairs.

One year during the joke camel racing at the Olympia show Ted Edgar persuaded the Irish Army rider Con Power to stand on a step ladder, and salute to the crowd before his camel was brought. However, they just left him up there throughout the whole routine.

At a contest in South Africa it was suggested to Iris Kellet, the Irish chef d'équipe, that Ted Edgar was sabotaging the chances of her boys by keeping them out late. She imposed a ten o'clock curfew, which the young Irishmen overcame in the time-honoured tradition of feigning sleep until the 'prefect' had been round, and then escaping. One evening Eddie Macken nearly concussed himself falling off a chair and had to be surreptitiously patched up the next day to ride.

Figure VII

The Ladies, God Bless 'Em

Woman power

'Psychologists have been known to write treatises on why
adolescent girls should be attracted to the horse. The reason
is simple. It provides an early outlet for the exercise of
power in preparation for the supreme tyranny of marriage
and motherhood.'   (Rintoul Booth)

Dam' fine sight

'There is nothing more pleasing than a good-looking horse
ridden side-saddle by a finished Horsewoman.'
                                    (*Modern Horsemanship*, 1937)

Personal remarks

'If you say to a pretty girl – "You have a nice seat" – she may very well slap your face. Try the same phrase on a horsewoman and her features will form into a radiant smile, as she replies, "I know".' (Rintoul Booth)

Men only

Show-jumping was first included in the Olympics in 1912 – where it was male only. It wasn't until 1956 that Pat Smythe was the first lady to ride at the Olympics.

Well, they were getting too good . . .

1948 was the last year the ladies could compete in the prestigious King George V Cup contest, since thereafter they had their own Queen Elizabeth Cup.

Ladies only

Since there is now no World or European Ladies Championship the Queen Elizabeth II Cup at the Royal International is the top competition restricted to lady riders.

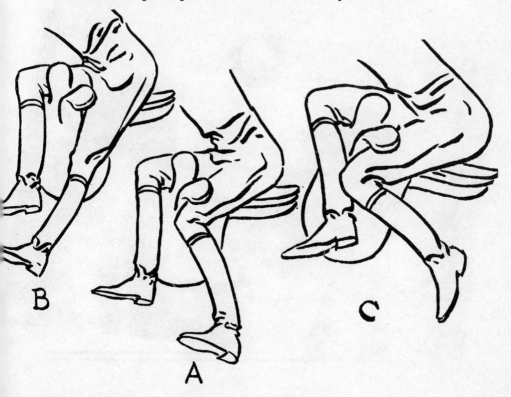

B

A

C

GLOSSARY

Dismounting. 'Involuntary dismounting is generally classified as a fall.' (Rintoul Booth)

Disunited. Falling off.

Gag. Something which Bob Hope pays other people to write for him.

Hack. A reporter from the *News of the World* asking Peter Robeson about hedgehog skins on his practice poles.

Interfering with your horse. Not yet an illegal offence.

Riding (1). 'The art of keeping a horse between yourself and the ground.' (Rintoul Booth)

Riding (2). 'One of the best exercises for the businessman who is forced to sit in an office most of the day.'

Tack. Bitless bridles are bridles without bits which may be:

(a) accidental

(b) on purpose

. . . In the case of (b) [the rider] may be a cowboy or a gaucho or someone who has been persuaded to buy a bitless bridle against his better judgement from a trade stand at Badminton.'

(c) tasteless goods

Jumping against the clock: variations on a theme
Withers. The effect of too much alcohol.
Stifle. What people do to yawns when watching showing classes.
Qualified for Wembley. Won an F.A. cup semi-final.
Rolling a top pole. Getting lucky in Warsaw.
Power and speed. Rolling a top pole against the clock.
Finding a sponsor. Getting someone to buy you a drink.
Have a sponsor. Will grovel.
Frog. A rider from across the Channel.
Curry Comb. An Indian headpiece.
Dandy Brush. What Beau Brummel used to do his hair.
Wisp. A chocolate bar with a bite out of it.
Body brush. For those with similar tendencies.
Chef d'equipe. Team cook.
Wing. Used sensibly with a 'prayer' can achieve spectacular results.
Seeing a stride. (Aus) finding half a pair of trousers.
Derby bank. Messrs Ladbroke, Hill & Coral.
Rapping. Illegal practice which involves coloured disc jockeys.

Top Ten

1. **I heard it through David Vine** — Smokey Robeson & the Miracles
2. **Father & Son** — The Smiths
3. **Jean Germany** — David Bowen
4. **Ticket to Ride** — Boy Phillips & Pony Club
5. **Wuthering Heights** — Gate, Brush
6. **Ain't no oxer higher enough** — Mr. Ross & The Supremes
7. **Roll over Beethoven** — Douglas Bunn with the Cyril Light Orchestra
8. **Can't get no good Hock Action** — The Rolling Poles
9. **Rock against the Clock** — Edgar & the Teds
10. **Take it to the Limit** — Wings

NEW ENTRIES:

When I'm 64 — David Broome
Goodbye Yellow Brick Wall — Alan Oliver Newton John
Knock on Wood — The Carpenters
Grease — Alan Ball and His Jazzmen

THE British Show Jumping Association is run by prunes, or so it looks. A BSJA hand-out of staff names comes my way and we have the perfect ingredients for a nursery rhyme. Reversing the rhyme, we have a sailor in the form of Lt Commander W. B. Jefferis, the secretary general, and there's a soldier, Colonel P. R. Drew, on the executive committee. And the chairman of the training committee is ... a Miss Tinka Taylor. What can her parents have been thinking of?

London Standard diary

KEVIN WOODCOCK

TRUE FACTS

The early bird steals a march

Competitors have been known to get up early in the morning when they think no one is watching and school their horses round the course which has been erected the night before – though this ploy hasn't always worked. One morning at Hickstead Ray Howe was trying this when he thought he saw someone approaching. In a panic he dismounted, untacked his horse, left it in the arena and scuttled off to bed, only to find out later that the approaching official was none other than a hat and coat hung up on the railings.

The late Gerald Barnes, a very popular judge, tended to turn a blind eye to this sort of thing, even though he used to park his caravan at the ringside. One competitor admitted to Gerald that he might need practice, to which Gerald replied that if he didn't get caught or make too much noise he would promise not to look out of his window. Later on that day Gerald rounded on the competitor and told him that he had made one hell of a din that morning, only to discover that the culprit had overslept and that someone else had been having a clandestine practice. Since Gerald was true to his word and hadn't looked, no one ever knew who it was!

The course builders, however, have got wise to these tricks and if they think someone has had a practice, will slightly change the fences. On other occasions riders have slightly modified the jumps to suit themselves overnight, without being discovered!

A little flutter

Though it still hasn't really caught on, gambling on show-jumping competitions was in evidence as early as the Madrid Show of 1951.

On a marathon show tour of Britain when the Whitaker brothers were young they were to cross the Forth Bridge, with Mrs Whitaker at the wheel. There was no one to accept the toll, so they drove on across, only to be stopped on the fr side and searched thoroughly by the police, who were investigating a recent bank robbery. All they found in the truck was two weeks' worth of dirty laundry.

At the start of Robert Smith's career he had three ponies entered at a show. On the first he went before the starter's bell, so was eliminated. On the second he missed fence four and was eliminated. On the third he missed fence six and was again eliminated. Harvey was understandably annoyed when the crowd booed as he quietly thumped his son.

Before the advent of the all-inclusive mega horsebox, many competitors travelled around with old caravans hitched on to the back of their wagons – often with the result that they were inadvertently left in ditches or showgrounds without the driver being remotely aware.

When Boomerang was winning so many classes lots of people started trying to emulate Eddie Macken by using a hackamore, or bitless bridle. Graham Fletcher got one, but just as he was about to enter the ring a fellow competitor told him he had put it on upside down. With a top rider like that getting it wrong, it's frightening to think how many novice riders must have made mistakes while trying blindly to copy their heroes.

Ted Edgar used to entertain friends with a mechanical rodeo machine.

David Broome is a joint master of the Curre Foxhounds.

Ted Edgar does a cabaret act.

Olympic jumper Ann Moore briefly took up motor racing.

Harvey Smith is an accomplished barbeque cook who makes his own sauces.

Malcolm Pyrah used to work in local government before joining Trevor Banks to become a show-jumper.

Harvey Smith first got his taste for being a public spectacle at the Bingley Gala of 1951 where he came second in a talent contest with his performing dog Lassie.

Lionel Dunning has in the past worked as a coalman, a truck driver, a car assembly worker and a farrier.

Caroline Bradley played hockey at County level.

Ted Edgar would seldom take Nick Skelton on horse-buying trips as he even managed to make rubbish look good.

To combat the heat at the Los Angeles Olympics each horse had an air-conditioning fan, and sprinklers on the roof helped to keep the stables cool. (In LA everything is COOL!)

The Royal International Horse Show returned for one nostalgic but disastrous year to the White City. The venue couldn't really cope with all the horses, half the arena was flooded one night when a hose was left on, and the gate control appeared to let in quite a high number of gate-crashers. The White City ground was sold the next year anyway, so the show moved to Birmingham.

The last day of the Horse of the Year Show is the official end of the show-jumping season, despite later shows like Olympia.

BRIDLES.

Our Special Cowboy Bridle.

No. 10K1700 Our Special Two-Ear Flat Russet Cowboy Bridle. ¾-inch double cheeks, adjustable on both sides, with large nickel ornament. Spotted crown piece with two ear holes. Weight, about 14 ounces.

Price of bridle without bit **$1.09**

For price on bridle reins see Nos. 10K1709, 10K1712 and 10K1713.
If by mail, postage extra, 18 cents.

Our $1.65 Cowboy Bridle.

No. 10K1701 Our Special Two-Ear Cowboy Bridle, with spotted face piece and fancy stamped scalloped cheeks, adjustable on each side. Nickel buckles and ornaments. Bridle is made out of russet oiled leather. Weight, about 16 ozs.

Price of bridle without bit..... **$1.65**

For price on bridle reins see Nos. 10K1709, 10K1712 and 10K1713.
For price on bit for bridle, see page 149.
If by mail, postage extra, 20 cents.

Our Great Western Bridle.

No. 10K1702 Our Great Western Cowboy Bridle, made with wide pointed fancy stamped cheek, adjustable crown and throat latch. Fancy stamped brow band. Nickel buckles and ornaments. One of the new, up to date Western bridles; ¾-inch by 6 feet reins, to loop in. Weight, about 24 ounces.

Price of bridle with bit.........**$2.72**
Without bit 2.38

If by mail, postage extra, 33 cents.

Braided Bridle Reins.

No. 10K1709 Our Special Braided Bridle Reins, made of fine quality calfskin, extra long with romal and quirt ends. These reins are made in three sizes: 4-plait, 6-plait and 8-plait. Weight, about 10 ounces.

Price, for 4-plait...............$1.13
Price, for 6-plait............... 1.45
Price, for 8-plait............... 1.81

Our Jack Frost Sleigh Bells.

We make this strap of sleigh bells on a good heavy 1-inch black harness leather strap, using 30 fine nickel plated pressed steel bells, 1½-inch diameter, riveted to the strap also make it with 30 1¼-inch nickel plated bells riveted to the strap. These two styles of sleigh bells are very popular and are considered great value. All the bells are finely nickel plated and all have clear ringing tone. Order Jack Frost Bells.

No. 10K7204 Price, per strap **$1.35**
of 30 1½-inch bells.
If by mail, postage extra, 36 cents.
No. 10K7207 Price, per strap **$1.50**
of 30 1¼-inch bells.
If by mail, postage extra, 48 cents.

Overcheck Bit.

No. 10K8330 Overcheck Bit, to be used as a separate bit on overdraw check reins. Weight, 3 oz. XO plate. Price, 2 for..... **8c**
Nickel plate. Price, 2 for..... **10c**
If by mail, postage extra, 4 cents.

Rubber Mouth Bit.

No. 10K8340 Squire's Flexible Rubber Mouth Bit, nickel, half cheek snaffle. Weight, 7 ozs. Each **29c**
If by mail, postage extra, 10 cents.

The Celebrated Humane Bit.

No. 10K8343 The Celebrated Humane Bit is made of solid leather, the strongest and best bit on the market, and can not pull through the mouth. With this bit you do not need any overdraw bit, the overdraw buckles in small rings, and pulls from under jaw, making it very easy on horse. Nickel plated rings. Weight, about 16 ounces. Price, each **65c**
If by mail, postage extra, 11 cents.

Our Straight Blade Horse or Mule Shear.

No. 10K4838 This Horse or Mule Shear is made with straight blades from the very best double shear cutlery steel, carefully hammer forged, and made the proper shape for hand shearing in roaching the mane, tail and fetlocks. Short blades, which make it easily handled. Blades are 4 inches long. Full length of shear, 9 inches. Weight of shear, 7 ounces. Price **33c**
If by mail, postage extra, 10 cents.

REDUCED PRICE ON CURRY COMBS.
Eight-Bar, Solid Back Curry Comb.

No. 10K4921 Our Leader in an eight bar solid back curry comb. Solid steel shank running through the handle and riveted. Made from cold rolled steel, pressed knockers, lacquered finish. steel shank and 12 ounces. Weight, about

Price, per dozen, $1.10; each **10c**
If by mail, postage extra, each, 14 cents.

Harness Soap.

No. 10K4348 Frank Miller's Harness Soap. This is without question the best harness soap made. By using it your harness will wear longer and look better. Weight, per cake, 12 ounces.

Price, each.................. **11c**
If by mail, postage extra, each, 14 cents.

Riding Cuffs.

No. 10K3175 Our Fine Western Riding Cuffs, fancy stamped body 7 inches long, lace body and one button at the wrist. This cuff is made of extra fine russet cuff leather, and will fit over the coat sleeve. Weight, about 10 ounces. Price, per pair, **$1.00**
If by mail, postage extra, per pair, 14 cents.

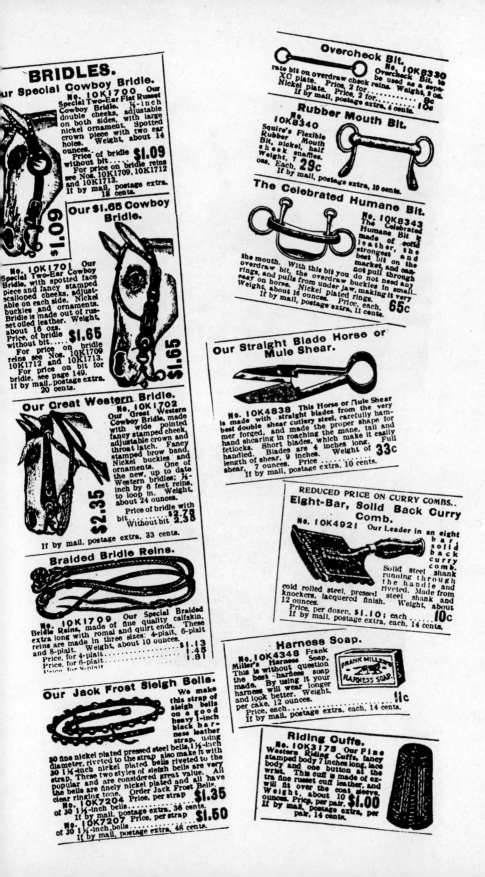

WITHOUT REINS.
CAPTAIN S. RODZIANKO WINNING A SHOW JUMPING COMPETITION IN VIENNA ON THE THOROUGHBRED ROSALINE.

How to be held up by a bank.

The Santa Canter, or equestrian break-dancing.

At the 1975 Easter Hickstead meeting the weather was so bad that all jumping was halted in the International Arena, but the riders had the added challenge of Douglas Bunn's newly-invented sport – cross-country team chasing, round a mile and a half of solid mid-Surrey drag fences.

When Caroline Bradley won her second Queen Elizabeth Cup, on Tigre in 1980, she was under intense pressure. She part-owned the horse with Mr Donald Bannocks, who claimed that he was not being sufficiently informed of the horse's movements. The horse was put up for sale by sealed tender, to be opened on the first day of that Royal International Show. The highest bid, being exactly twice as high as any others, £160,000, came from Mr Bannocks himself. Caroline didn't intend giving Mr Bannocks £80,000 for her share, so the horse became his sole property.

All was resolved, however, by the end of the week, when Mr Bannocks paid Caroline £80,000 and also let her keep the ride. This didn't last long though, and Tigre was sold and sent to Paddy McMahon.

During the ownership wrangles over Tigre a ten year-old fan sent Caroline Bradley £10 towards buying the horse for her heroine.

It was only by chance that John Whitaker got the ride on Ryan's Son. His father always wanted to buy it, but it was beyond the family budget. Mr Whitaker discussed the horse with a chap called Donald Oates who persuaded the owner – Mrs Wright – to let him, Donald, ride Ryan at a few shows. Mr Oates then bought the horse. Father Whitaker still wanted the horse for John, and when poor Donald Oates was suffering from piles he let John have the ride. The combination immediately clicked and Mr Whitaker persuaded another of their previous owners, Mr Barr, to buy the horse for John. (The Whitakers chipped in one fifth of the asking price as a token of their faith in the horse.)

Dorian Williams was heard to remark when told that the cup for the *Daily Mail* Pony Club Games was festooned with ribbons, 'Don't worry, Lady Rothermere is presenting it and she's dressed the same way.'

In 1953 at the Horse of the Year Show at Harringay Alan Oliver took the first four places in the Leading Showjumper of the Year championships and was also sixth and seventh.

VITAL STATISTICS

In 1937, Colonel Rodzianko wrote in *Modern Horsemanship:*

'The head should be of medium dimensions and the forehead broad between the eyes, as this is a sign of brains. The eye should be full and have a wide range of vision. It must be well set. A good expression shows a good disposition. The ears should be well pricked up and not too large' – Sorry, David Broome!

'The chest should be as deep as possible. A deep chest carries the girths well. It should be broad as it contains the breathing organs' – Good for Samantha Foxhunting.

'The hips should be large. This is very important for jumping.'

TONY: AGED 42

Correct feeding is important. Your horse should not look like this.

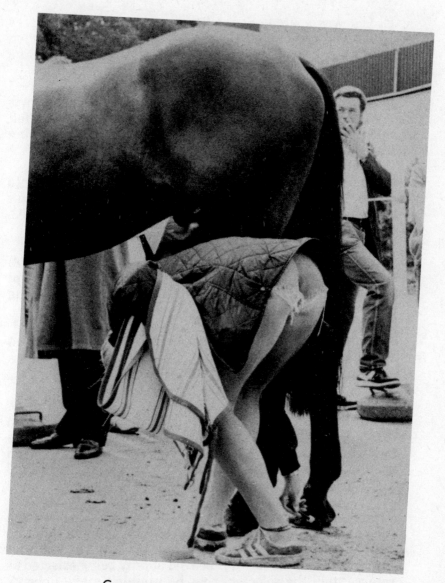

Grooms used to wear jackets and cloth caps.

'The thighs must be well-covered with muscle.'

A good groom should be 'clean, disciplined, respectful, honest and sober'.

'El Cid was a great Spanish hero and [another] military leader who accomplished what so many English horsemen do without any conscious effort – appear to be dead from the neck up.' (Rintoul Booth)

John Whitaker is very superstitious: he used to keep parts of bridles associated with success almost until they fell apart, and used to warm up in the same part of a collecting ring at a show where he'd been previously successful.

Is John Whitaker as boring as he looks? No – according to one of his owners, Fred Brown, as quoted in John's biography: 'He can be quite mischievous when he's out with the lads.' Wow!

According to one of John Whitaker's friends, jumper Geoff Billington, no one has a bad word to say about him except that when he's at the bar he seems to have very long pockets and very short arms.

Alan Oliver's early style of riding, where he would almost throw himself at the fence, gave rise to the saying: 'It's a good horse which can follow Alan Oliver.'

When Lionel Dunning's son Robert was born he quite naturally went out on the tiles, forgetting to a certain extent that his wife Pam had had anything to do with the happening. As a reminder of this on Robert's birthday, Pam opens a bottle of bubbly to drink with the nanny, and Lionel is excluded.

After Robert Smith had become the youngest man to win the King George V Cup at the Royal International show, he was, as tradition dictated, offered a place in the team for Dublin. Harvey, somewhat peeved at only being selected as reserve, told the selectors that he wouldn't make Robert's horses available for the Dublin trip. This in effect promoted Harvey from reserve to full team member. Harvey apparently didn't want Robert put under too much pressure so early in his career!

Caroline Bradley had what she felt were embarrassingly large hands and used to sit on them when talking to people.

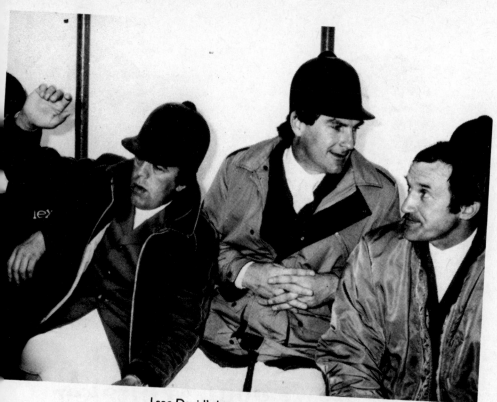

I see David's been at the pints again!

THE DACHSHORSE.

Raymond Brooks-Ward interviews John Whitaker for TV

RBW: Well done John — a marvellous win

JW: Er. . . Yep, great, Raymond

RBW: That makes you leading rider of the show

JW: Er. . . Yep

RBW: What Next?

JW: Was that a joke?

RBW: And now back to the studio

*(do they get paid
for that? — Ed)*

ONLY
£169.95

A HINT FOR FUTURE HORSE SHOWS.

IF YOU CAN'T HAVE ENGLISH JUMPS, WHY NOT MAKE YOUR CHOICE OF OBSTACLES FAIRLY INTERNATIONAL?

Harvey Smith bareback jumping.

🞒🞒🞒🞒🞒🞒🞒🞒🞒🞒 🞒🞒🞒🞒🞒🞒🞒🞒🞒🞒🞒🞒🞒🞒🞒

THE NATIONS CUP

The Prince Philip Trophy is awarded to the World team champions, based on each country's six Nations Cup results. The team for each Nations Cup can alter.

A Nations Cup contest is run over two rounds. Any British rider who manages a double clear is awarded a coveted new red coat.

In 1982 the BSJA ran out of funds to send teams to Nations Cup competitions, but, undeterred, and with official blessing, a 'private' team of Fred Welch, Pam and Lionel Dunning, and Sally Mapleson set off to Spain. The Spanish authorities were very helpful and promised that if the British won, they would foot the bills. They did and they did.

At one evening performance at Madrid for a Nations Cup competition in 1954 the class didn't finish until 3:30 am.

In Nations Cup classes the speed required not to incur time faults has changed dramatically from the early days. In the Fifties the required pace was 280 yards per minute. Today it is 436 yards per minute.

CAUTION TO YOUNG LADIES WHO RIDE IN CRINOLINE ON DONKEYS.

As a horse grows older and older, its teeth become longer and yellower till its mouth looks like the keyboard of a pub piano. If the teeth work up and down, it may be a pub piano.

'Swimming' a horse during a drought.

HORSEY.

Little Alfred (in Papa's coat and cap,. "HOW DO YOU LIKE MY NEW HORSE, GEORGE?"
Cousin George. "UM!—HE'S A GOODISH TOPP'D 'UN. BUT—AWFULLY COARSE SHOULDER, AND TOO THICK IN THE HOCKS AND PASTERNS!"

HORSEPLAY

Boomerang was a relatively unsound horse for most of his life and had been de-nerved – an operation which effectively numbs the lower part of the leg – but nevertheless won four successive Hickstead Jumping Derbys.

Early in the career of Ryan's Son, the horse broke a small tip off a bone in his foot. After an operation he made a full recovery and the inch square sliver of bone is now bottled as a souvenir.

Between 1975 and 1985 Ryan's Son jumped for Britain 34 times in the double-round Nations Cup competitions and had 34 clear rounds.

Andrew Fielder became famous for his horse Vibart, a sturdy individual who occasionally used to give out a kick after clearing a jump. By coincidence Andrew once tried to buy Ryan's Son, a horse with very similar characteristics, but the vet didn't pass the horse sound – he had a couple of lumps on his hindlegs below the hock, called curbs, which to this day have never caused the horse any problems.

On one international trip the 17hh Foxhunter had to be quietly persuaded to bend his knees on entering the aircraft since the door was only 16hh high.

The horse Forever won the Queen's Cup in 1979, was second in 1980, and won it again in 1981 and 1982.

The reason why most German horses' tails are unattractively shaved at the top of the dock is that tail 'pulling' is not allowed in Germany as it is thought cruel.

PLATE 42.—*Excellent example of left leg and foot in correct position when jumping.*

The games mentioned by Miss Peck are described here. If words fail the diagrams will help you out!

CRUSTS AND CRUMBS

Mounted teams face one another approximately eight yards apart. Behind each team a line is marked approximately ten yards from the tails of the horses. Each team is named either 'Crusts' or 'Crumbs' and they await the shout of either name from a third party. If 'Crusts' is called, 'Crumbs' have to chase them and touch them before they escape across the safety line ('Crusts Home'). Captured 'Crusts' have to stay in jail until their team is eliminated. The more advanced the riders, the wider apart the safety lines can be.

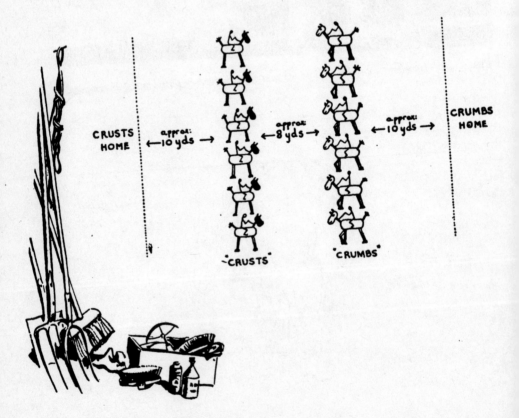

CRUSTS HOME   ← approx: 10 yds →   ← approx: 8 yds →   ← approx: 10 yds →   CRUMBS HOME

'CRUSTS'   'CRUMBS'

TWOS AND THREES

This is played exactly like the game of the same name which you must have played on foot. But instead of standing one in front of the other, the ponies stand side by side.

A circle is made with ponies in pairs. One rider is 'he' who chases another. In order not to be caught, riders are permitted to go anywhere (within limits!) and not only inside and outside the circle formed by the pairs, but dodging in and out of the circle. As soon as a pair becomes three, the *outside* rider of the trio has to escape and make a trio elsewhere. And so on.

RIDE AND TIE

Teams are made up in pairs (any number of 'pairs' can take part), number one mounted and number two unmounted. Number one gallops round a post, dismounts and ties up pony to another post placed half-way back to number two. He (or she) runs back to number two and passes over the handkerchief. Number two runs to the pony, unties it, mounts and gallops back to his team and touches the second couple who carry on as before. It's a sort of glorified relay race. Whichever team finishes first wins. *One important point: instead of using posts it is better to have somebody to hold the pony. It's safer than tying up.*

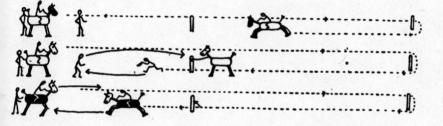

Some unscrupulous riders use undetectable drugs to enhance their horses' performance. The drugs look like this.

A HORSE BY ANY OTHER NAME

As commercialism has increased over the years the somewhat muddling situation has arisen of horses having their names changed, sometimes more than once. This has occasionally got out of hand. A gelding had its name changed to Elizabeth Ann, and Harvey Smith has had two horses called Sanyo Sweet Music. Here are some other examples, with occasional stable names in brackets.

Pele = Kerry Gold

Olympic Star = Sanyo Sanmar

Dudley Boy = **Upton** (*a former Wembley champion working hunter*) = Sanyo Video

Doncella = Mattie Brown

Cropello = Mr Ross

Tiayo = Union Jack

Spectator II = Ganderbush = Jungle Bunny (Tarzan)

Abor = Graffiti = Sanyo Music Centre

Sunnyside Up = Harris Home Care

Epsom = Everest If Ever

In the early days of TV coverage the producer often used to plug into the live PA system for his commentary.

Many riders feel that the atmosphere of the Wembley Shows has declined since the building of the hotel next to the stadium, which resulted in the demise of the 'caravan village' where all the riders used to stay.

1954 – Colonel Mike Ansell: 'The growing popularity of show-jumping has led some critics to suggest that the sport, which until recently was restricted to a select few, is now being commercialized.'

How methods change: 'A rider must remember to keep . . . "heels down, toes out, knees in, hollowed back . . ."'   *Modern Horsemanship,* 1937

The timing schedules of an early international TV broadcast led the BBC in 1954 to broadcast almost an entire programme devoted to the building of a puissance course, followed by only a couple of rounds before they went off the air.

In 1985 there were

1605 shows
2405 show days

with

prize money totalling

£1,405,397

301,712 starters

with

TOTAL MEMBERSHIP OF BSJA 14,519

Showjumping is an exciting spectator sport.

EXTRACT FROM

Silly Cooper's *JUMPERS*: Page 4,307

as Kevin buckled up his belt, pulled on his T-shirt and his Cuban-heeled boots, Samantha lay back on the bunk in the lorry and pulled the rumpled duvet up to her chin. Her face was glowing from the after effects of their vigorous love-making, and also because Kevin hadn't shaved for two days. She couldn't bring herself to believe the rumours that this glorious bit of 'rough trade' was having an affair with Peter Hetherington-Forsyth, the assistant team vet. Nevertheless when Kevin had been a 'lad' at a racing stable in Lambourn it was said he 'ran under both sets of rules'.

Over the years Hickstead, had always been a happy place for Samantha. She'd won some of her best classes there and back in 1980 she'd worked her way through the entire Irish and German teams, which was some achieve-ment for a three-day show.

Since Kevin had come to work as her groom, her life had changed dramatically. Samantha had always had a very good relationship with her sponsors, since she'd had a very good relationship with their chairman, but now all this had changed.

'I'm just off to do the horses,' said Kevin. 'What if he gets caught,' thought Samantha, as she drifted back to sleep. After about ten minutes she was wakened by the clunk of a door. She rolled over and saw Margaret Brogue, the woman who had instructed her from her Pony Club days and who had taught her all she knew. Her stubble was worse than Kevin's.

'Morning Sam.'

'What do you want?'

'I've just popped in to pick up the new batteries for you electric numnah. By the way I'm a bit worried about that

concoction that Peter made up for Prince – I tried some myself and I've only just come down.'

'Well, for God's sake tell Kevin to go easy with it when he does the feeds.'

'Margaret sat down on the edge of the bunk and put her arm around Samantha. 'I've got two tickets for the Ladies Final at Wimbledon and I've booked a room at the Van Dyke Hotel – I know it's the week before Wembley, but do come.'

Samantha was in a dilemma. She dearly wanted to be selected for the European Championships and had already planned a secret evening with the Chairman of the Selectors – a retired Colonel who had once been in a British team, when it was only open to 'officers and gentlemen.' How times had changed.'

'I'll think about it.'

Samantha got up and turned off the kettle. Her mind was now on how she could win the important class that afternoon. The other competitors were riding a bit below par and if she could go clear in the first round, the speed jump-off would be a formality.

The door opened just a few centimetres and a large brown envelope slid across the floor. Samantha opened it and found a note and £500 in old tenners. 'Have a refusal in the first round' the note said 'and

Old-fashioned horses always used to gallop with their forelegs stretched out in front and their hindlegs out the back – that was until the camera was invented, when they learned how to do it properly.

PEOPLE

Arriving late at night for a show, Caroline Bradley found a length of wire to tie the doors of the less than adequate stabling. The next morning she discovered it was connected to the PA system.

German show-jumper Fritz Ligges won a team bronze for eventing in the Tokyo Olympics.

Harry Llewellyn had several rides in the Grand National.

John Whitaker was in the Rockwood Harriers Pony Club Event Team.

Pat (Koechlin) Smythe was the first woman chef d'équipe (team manager), in 1967.

Caroline Bradley was the first woman to win the puissance (high jump) at the Horse of the Year Show in 1974, but it took her 12 attempts to win the Queen Elizabeth Cup, which she eventually did on Marius in 1978.

In 1978 Caroline Bradley was the first woman to ride in the newly 'open' world championships.

Pat Smythe and Harry Llewellyn were immortalized by Madame Tussaud's.

Pat Smythe carried an Olympic torch on horseback for part of the distance from Malmo to Stockholm.

Raimondo d'Inzeo, younger than his look-alike brother Piero, became a member of the Italian mounted police after leaving the cavalry and competing for Italy at the 1948 Olympics. He subsequently won an individual silver at the Stockholm games in 1956 and the gold in Rome four years later. He also rode at the Montreal games at the age of 51. The two brothers were still winning top classes in 1982, when a pupil of the Schockemöhles, having no idea who the d'Inzeos were, remarked that they weren't bad for a couple of old Army boys.

THE WAY WE WERE . . .

One of the earliest protagonists, Lt Col W.E. Lyon, was once asked to jump-judge at Olympia. 'I shall never forget the agony of mind and body that I endured,' he wrote. 'Either I was not in training for it or had had too late a night before and/or too large a lunch, but after an hour and a half of uneventful, slow-motion jumping, my eyelids refused to function normally and not even the crashing of jumps nor the plaudits of the crowd could keep me awake; I was, to all intents and purposes a somnambulist in a top hat.' He managed somehow to give a rider who had obviously gone clear 'half a fault by my subconscious self, and so pandemonium reigned'. Fortunately his counterfoil gave a clear verdict, but Col Lyon was relieved never to be asked to judge again.

Show-jumping was first included at Olympic level in 1912 – at the Paris Games of 1900 there had been a high jump and long jump equestrian contest, known then as prize jumping.

The British Show Jumping Association was started in 1922 by Lt Col 'Taffy' Walwyn, the Glencross brothers and Frank Alison. The first Chairman-Secretary was Dorian Williams's father, Col V.D.S. 'Pudding' Williams. Another early stalwart was 'Bogey' Bowden-Smith. The first ace course designer in those days was Phil Blackmore. Its membership stood at 112. The following year it had increased to 197 and had £205 in the bank. In 1985 the membership total was 14,519, there were 1,605 affiliated shows, consisting of 2,405 days' jumping, with 301,712 starters and prize money totalling £1,405,397.

Between the wars there were two distinct types of show-jumping contest – those for the military and those for civilian dealers to show off their wares. They almost became two rival sports. It was only with the abolition of the cavalry schools at the end of the war that the two sports mixed.

How to kick off a top rail before attempting an oversized obstacle.

Blatant advertising has always been controversial in equestrian pursuits.

'Horse dealers make used car salesmen look positively honest.' – Traditional quote

'Show-jumping itself need not be the sole object of human effort and existence. Indeed, it is not my intention to die an old maid – not even gloriously – in the middle of an international show ring.'   *Pat Smythe, 1954*

Liz Edgar: 'Now, if we had a high-calibre horse, at the first sign of him going lame, I would have him de-nerved.'

Dorian Williams, writing about commentating, in the Fifties: 'Sometimes a commentator is tempted to become a "turn" in himself . . . This is quite reprehensible.'

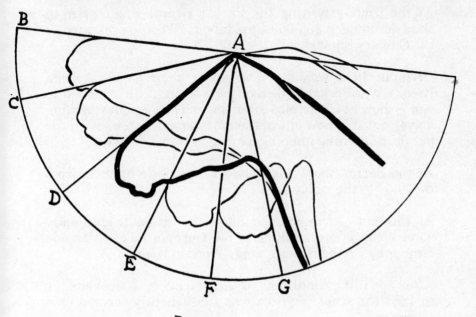

DIAGRAM D

Positions of Horse's Head.

A-D—*Ideal (natural) position.*

A-E—*Intermediate position between the natural and the collected.*

A-F—*Perpendicular to the ground, typical of collection.*

A-G—*Extreme bent position.*

A-C—*Extension in maximum effort.*

A-B—*Star-gazing.*

★ ★ ★ ★ ★ ★ ★ ★ ★ ★ ★ ★ ★ ★ ★ ★ ★ ★ ★ ★

Showbiz

In 1983 British Equestrian Promotions handled nearly £1,500,000 of sponsorship involving over 40 companies.

At the time of writing the world's richest single prize in show-jumping is $35,000 Can. (about £20,000) presented at the Calgary Show.

Olympia 1972 was the first major show that Raymond Brooks-Ward organized. Everyone thought he was mad to run a show at Christmas after the end of the show-jumping 'term', but it is now one of the most popular shows with the public, combining jumping, pantomime and displays.

At the Berlin Show riders used to commute by train from the hotel to the stable area.

At the end of the Aachen Show the crowd traditionally wave clean white hankies to the German folk tune made famous by Elvis Presley's song, 'Wooden Heart'.

After appalling conditions in the practice ring at Wembley in 1981 the schooling area was subsequently covered by a marquee.

The German team won the Olympic gold medal at Munich in 1972 by ¼ of a time fault from the USA.

At the Northampton, British Timken Show there was a class called the BSJA Olympic Trial. This was a somewhat strange name since it happened every year, and often after the Olympics.

Veteran jumper of the Fifties Ted Williams now trains greyhounds.

★ ★ ★ ★ ★ ★ ★ ★ ★ ★ ★ ★ ★ ★ ★ ★ ★ ★ ★

Hugo Simon using aerodynamics to assist his flight.

The social scene

'The gymkhanas were an amusing, revealing slice of wartime country life among horse lovers. One had to be extremely tactful, for there were delicate balances of prestige, social niceties, snobberies and jealousies and numerous examples of those old, proud, touchy elements in the character of the English lady busy as a bee as she organizes her country fêtes, her garden parties, her summer "season" of charity events.'

(Pat Smythe, *Jump for Joy,* 1954)

Putting on the style . . .

'Style is much more than appearance; it goes deeper than mere looks, and, as the late Count Görtz used to say – is more important than victory.'

(Piero Santini, *The Forward Impulse,* 1937)

Mad dogs and Englishmen . . .

During a minor 'cold war' crisis in Berlin a Russian observer apparently reported back to his supervisor that the Americans were dashing about threatening to push the button, the French were ready to fight to the last man, and the British were busy organizing a horse show.

Jam tomorrow . . .

Show-jumpers are liable to cash-flow problems. Some entry fees for shows have to be paid up to three months beforehand and are liable to VAT, but prize money may not arrive until two or three months after the event.

Gym-Khana

Exercises for the rider: 'After having had a hot bath, let out the water and sponge the body with cool or cold water. A cold sponge should be used between each exercise. Begin the physical drill: Exercise I – Place hands on either side of the bath, push the legs backwards, hollow the back and lift both legs straight forward, then swing the legs gently back . . . Exercise III – Stand erect in the bath . . .'

(*Modern Horsemanship*, 1937)

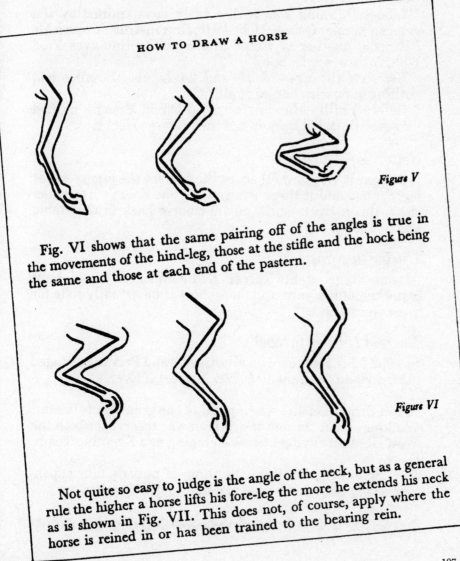

HOW TO DRAW A HORSE

Figure V

Fig. VI shows that the same pairing off of the angles is true in the movements of the hind-leg, those at the stifle and the hock being the same and those at each end of the pastern.

Figure VI

Not quite so easy to judge is the angle of the neck, but as a general rule the higher a horse lifts his fore-leg the more he extends his neck as is shown in Fig. VII. This does not, of course, apply where the horse is reined in or has been trained to the bearing rein.

PEOPLE

A good mix . . .

One of Lionel Dunning's owners was a certain Ken Wood of kitchen appliance fame. Ken started the popular Stocklands Equestrian Centre near Liphook, Hants, which over the years has been run by several well-known equestrian personalities, including at one time Badminton winner Celia Ross-Taylor.

Lionel Dunning was in his early days trained by the veteran jumper George Hobbs. His first instructor was a Mr Paterson, another of whose pupils at the time was Fred Welch's future wife, Sue.

Between the ages of 17 and 24 Lionel Dunning had nothing to do with horses at all.

Before Phillip Harris sponsored David Broome he had horses with David Barker and then George Hobbs.

Better safe than sorry . . .

Liz Edgar is very careful about the courses she jumps on her top horses, and if there is anything she doesn't like when she walks a track, she'll put her horse back in the stable and not jump.

Under two flags . . .

At one stage of his career Eddie Macken joined Paul Schockemöhle's yard and for a short time actually rode for West Germany.

Everest If Ever forever

In 1982 Nick Skelton won all three Grand Prix to be staged at Hickstead on the same horse, Everest If Ever.

Alwin Schockemöhle was a pupil of the great Hans Günter Winkler and at the age of nineteen was reserve for both the West German Olympic Show-Jumping and Eventing Team.

Paul Schockemöhle thinks nothing of putting four expensive newly-acquired horses into one single loose box.

It takes two to tango – John Whitaker and Ryan's Son take the floor.

What did the moron say when they told him he was putting a saddle on backwards?

"How do you know which way I'm going?"

TRUE FACTS

The golden rule

Since rules in most sports are arrived at by committee, show-jumpers, along with many other sportsmen, feel that the old adage that an ideal committee consists of two people, one of whom is ill on the day of the meeting, should apply!

The Pro-Am question: plus ça change

'Personally, I think the time has come when we all should agree that whether a rider be an amateur or professional, if he rides with skill or courage, he should be allowed to represent his country.' (Colonel Mike Ansell, 1954)

Apart from Olympic status, one current difference between 'amateur' and 'professional' jumpers is that 'amateurs' get paid in cash and professionals by cheque.

To keep in with the somewhat controversial 'amateur' rulings, former World Champion Gert Wiltfang was officially described as a car park attendant to allow him to compete at the 1972 Olympics.

Caroline Bradley was declared 'professional' in 1972, but although she appealed her classification was upheld, so she never achieved her greatest ambition of riding at the Olympics.

To retain their 'amateur' status the Whitaker brothers, though heavily sponsored, call themselves 'farmers'.

Pro-am/1956: Pat Smythe won a prize at school at the age of 8 for writing an essay called 'How to train a pony'. She wrote in her second autobiography, *One Jump Ahead* in 1956: 'No doubt if this most clear and instructive work had been published I would now be termed a professional rider!'

Never look a gift horse in the mouth – you may discover Schockemöhles.

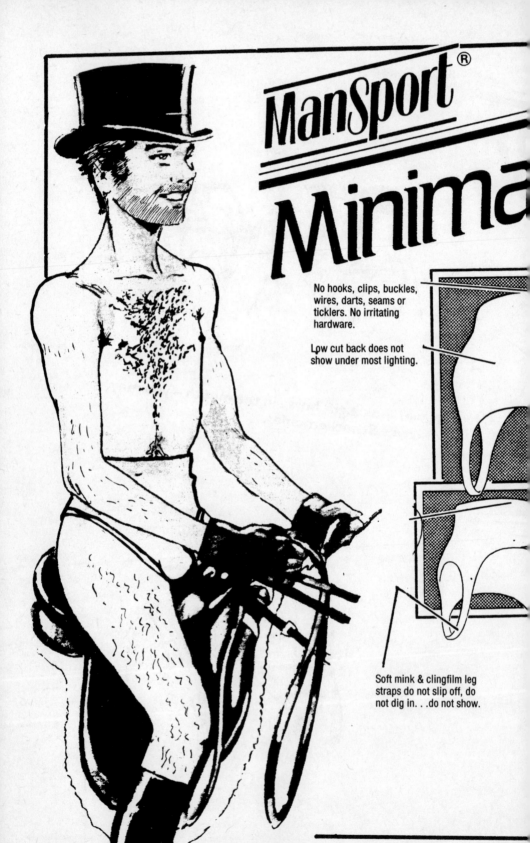

ManSport ®

Minima

No hooks, clips, buckles, wires, darts, seams or ticklers. No irritating hardware.

Low cut back does not show under most lighting.

Soft mink & clingfilm leg straps do not slip off, do not dig in. . .do not show.

The Ladies, God Bless 'Em

Men only
In 1954 Pat Smythe set off to the World Championships in Madrid only to discover when she got there that women riders were ineligible.

Vive la différence
Remarking on a coach trip in Spain in 1955, Pat Smythe wrote: 'The four-hour bus journey is worth recording and the passengers were very different from those one would meet on a London to Cheltenham run' – a very acute observation!

Distance no object
Caroline Bradley once did a television advertisement for Blue Band margarine. Since it was filmed in the winter the producers flew her to America because they wanted leaves in the shot.

The show must go on . . .
When Lionel Dunning had his nearly fatal fall at the Greater London Horseshow in 1975, his wife Pam was waiting in the wings, next to go. There was little she could do the following day at Balham Hospital, so she went back to the show and rode the same horse, Union Jack, in the class for which he was entered.

Difference between show-jumping and sex —
In show-jumping you enter, then declare. . .

THE WAY WE WERE

With style being the criterion in the early days, no faults were given for refusals. After 3 refusals, however, it was thought that the crowd might get bored, so the rider was politely asked to try another fence.

In the early 1900s it was quite permissible to circle in front of a fence, without penalty. If a rider felt his horse wasn't on the correct stride he was quite at liberty to veer him off at the last minute. Accuracy counted – time didn't.

In the early days of jumping, fences often had thin slats of wood resting on the top pole. A rider incurred faults if one of these should fall – though often the wind was the culprit.

In the infancy of the sport, the rules tended to be made up while the competition was in progress. The local Master of Foxhounds was usually the judge. Contests were often won by 'a damn-good-feller to hounds' after a dashing but disastrous performance. Once, a well-known MFH was judging at a show and his great friend, Fred Foster, a pioneer of the sport, had quite clearly finished second to a practically unknown combination. The MFH asked Fred what he ought to do. Fred said, 'Send us again.' They did, but Fred was again beaten. The judge didn't know what to do until Fred suggested that he make them go again and again until he actually did beat his rival. After two more rounds Fred eventually triumphed.

In France part of the Tote revenue from horse-racing is put towards their show-jumping team.

Show-jumping achieved its peak of TV popularity in the early Seventies when it used to be shown in the 9:20 slot and achieved audiences of between 11 and 12 million. Since then the sports scheduling has changed and popularity slightly declined.

Shakespearian way of controlling a horse: 'Woe, Woe and thrice Woe.'

(a) *From a Chinese scroll.*

(b) *French 17th Century hobby horse.*

How to ride trotting poles.

One of Ted Edgar's point-to-point owners got so emotional when Ted won a race for him that he started to cry when presented with the cup and his false teeth fell out.

During the ride past the Royal Box at the Stockholm Olympics several horses started playing up. Bill Steinkraus of the USA had a lucky escape when his horse reared up in front of the Queen, slipped over backwards and deposited Bill on the grass.

When Harvey Smith was put in touch with Sanyo by British Equestrian Promotions director Raymond Brooks-Ward, he had never heard of them, and confused them with Sony. Fortunately he was sufficiently briefed in time to avoid what could have prevented one of the most successful sponsorship deals in the sport.

How not to ride trotting poles.

Britain's only Olympic gold medal for show-jumping was won at Helsinki in 1952 with the legendary team of Harry Llewellyn (Foxhunter), Wilf White (Nizefela) and Dougie Stewart (Aherlow). It could be said that this victory almost led to the creation of show-jumping as we know it today. Up to 1984, in 10 Olympic Games, only once, in 1976, did the British jumpers come home without some sort of medal, and even that year Debbie Johnsey only just missed out by coming 4th.

It took course builders some time to get the correct amount of blue dye into their water fences, to give the right colour effect without ruining the breeches of any rider who was unlucky enough to get wet.

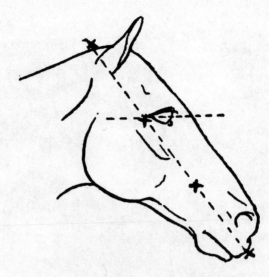

Figure IV. Eye one-third distance from poll. Note the angle of the eye to the line of the face

For the first two years of his life Robert Smith slept in a stable.

While hacking to the Richmond Show, as a child in 1939, Pat Smythe jumped the park benches for practice before going on to win her class.

Michael Caine's daughter Nikki was a top Show Jumper — Not a lot of people know that.

François Mathy once employed a vet to come and de-nerve a couple of his horses, but the vet went to the wrong set of stables and de-nerved the wrong horses.

Having recovered from his first serious fall, Lionel Dunning then broke his knee. While in hospital he used to 'escape' to the consulting rooms near Marble Arch to see Bill Tucker, who specializes in putting broken jockeys back together. On the way back from one of these clandestine trips he unfortunately found himself on the Tube sitting opposite the Matron from St Luke's, where he was meant to be!

Harvey Smith's driving ban for being over the limit has enabled him to sleep while on the road, and Robert now has to do all the work.

ROSETTES AND RIDERS

To the young, then, lies the responsibility of carrying into the future the torch of equestrianism and the care and training of the horse. This great horse show is the culmination of a showing season which, properly used, can be a means to this end. I am glad to be able to record my confidence that youth will not fail.

In 22 years of the Hickstead Derby only sixteen horses have jumped a clear round. The course has been the same each time.

On the selection committee for the Olympics have been riders such as David Broome, Malcolm Pyrah, Graham Fletcher and Peter Robeson.

In the finals of a World Championship competition the riders jump the first round on their own horses and then have to ride all their opponents' mounts.

Tranquillizers have been used to calm over-excited horses, and during a purge by the American authorities in 1978 twenty-two of their riders were found to have used them. Fines and bans were imposed in an attempt to clean up the sport.

THE WAY WE WERE

In 1947 a British military team won the Aga Khan Trophy at Dublin. Their unexpected win was achieved on horses captured from Germany.

Though Peter Robeson is thought of as one of the veteran riders from the early days of the sport (his first British team appearance was in 1947), his father was also in the British team before him.

1954 – Mrs Rockwell writing about jumping in South Africa: 'It is hoped that it will not be long before South Africa sends an Equestrian Team to the Olympic Games.'!

Show-jumping was one of the first sports to become a TV favourite in the early 50s.

Show-jumping might never have become so popular in Britain had it not been for the election of a socialist government in 1945. This somewhat bizarre speculation can easily be explained. In 1947 Britain's coal pits were nationalized and the owners bought out, one of whom was a young Welshman who then decided to concentrate wholly on his other enthusiasm, show-jumping. It was to a great extent his devotion to the sport and subsequent success that jumping flourished. His name – Harry Llewellyn.

It was Mike Ansell's idea to introduce 'barber pole' striped fences – which are now almost universal.

The first British civilian team to go abroad went to Nice and Rome in 1947 and consisted of Lt Col Harry Llewellyn, Bobbie Hall, Tom Brake, 'Curly' Beard and Bay Lane. They weren't very successful and were amused to overhear the authorities at Nice discussing what they could do to help Great Britain win a competition. Very soon, however, Britain entered its first golden age of show-jumping.

Napoleon's favourite charger, Marengo, was a 14.1 hh Arab.

The growth of jumping in Britain had much to do with the popularity of the Victory Championships held at the White City in 1945 and organized by Colonel Mike Ansell.

In 1977 a sort of Riders Union was formed called 'The International Riders Club'.

OOPS!

Team manager Ronnie Massarella emerges from the undergrowth with Debbie Johnsey.

'It is, as the old cliché puts it, a great life if you don't weaken. Given a constitution robust enough to support four hours' travel, all-day and all-evening show-jumping, midnight supper and a two am party, followed by a hundred-mile drive home in the horsebox – and still be in time for early morning service on a Sunday – there is indeed no reason for weakening, especially at the age of twenty-five.'!   (Pat Smythe, *Jump for Joy*)